Sea Kayak Navigation Simplified

Lee Moyer

ALPEN
BOOKS
PRESS

Published by
AlpenBooks Press, LLC
3616 South Rd, Ste C1
Mukilteo, WA 98275 USA
Telephone 425-290-8587

Manufactured in the United States of America
Illustrations: Jason Mohr
Book and cover design: Marge Mueller, Gray Mouse Graphics
Cover photo: Rippin' Productions—Jock Bradley
Book photos: Rippin' Productions—Jock Bradley; Lee Moyer

WARNING: Sea kayaking, like other outdoor activities, is inherently dangerous, due to the skills needed and the hostile environments encountered. Paddlers should take this into account, and should be aware of their abilities and limitations, and never paddle beyond them. The reader of this book should develop these navigation techniques under controlled conditions. The reader must also acquire the necessary kayak-handling skills to complement the navigation techniques described in this book.

TABLE OF CONTENTS

Navigating a kayak in the real world is never boring.

FOREWORD

I asked Lee Moyer to write this book sixteen months ago. My motivation was my own experience with sea kayak navigation . . . bad. Or, more to the point, nil. I have been a sea kayaker for fifteen years. Most of my paddling has been in the Puget Sound area, but I have kayaked along the coasts of British Columbia, Maine, Connecticut, and North Carolina, and in the Sea of Cortez. In all this time, I have never learned how to navigate on my own. I've always gone by the "seat of my pants" or have relied on another paddler to navigate. Sometimes the other person has known what he is doing, sometimes not.

It's not from a lack of trying that I hadn't learned navigation. I'd read the books, or at least tried to…boring. The problem with most navigation instruction books, whether they are for water or land, is that the authors provide more info, in greater detail, than most of us want to know. And let's face it, the subject really isn't that interesting. Until now, that is.

In my mind, Lee Moyer was the obvious person to write this book. I bought my first kayak at his store in 1985, and immediately took his basic sea kayaking techniques course. I will never forget his response when one of my fellow students asked him when we were going to learn how to roll a kayak (it's a male thing, wanting to roll a kayak before you've even learned how to paddle one). Lee's response, if I remember correctly, was, "Why would you want to roll a large, loaded kayak? Let's first learn to stay out of trouble. The best stuff is close to shore, anyway." Practical advice for this novice kayaker then, and still practical now.

Another reason Lee was the obvious person to write the book was his experience teaching navigation courses and writing articles for *Canoe & Kayak* magazine. He has a way of presenting complex techniques simply, without a lot of jargon. Lee's writing here is direct and conversational, much like his class presentations. He even includes some puns and bad jokes, just like in his classes.

It is now winter as I write this foreword. Reading Lee's manuscript makes me want to rush right out and try the techniques he describes. I think you'll want to do that, too.

Robert Koch
January 2001

PREFACE

Ever since my first kayak trip along Vancouver Island's west coast in 1969, I have thoroughly enjoyed exploring the rich coastline of the ocean. At that time, fiberglass sea kayaks were relatively new and techniques were very basic. I was taught the fundamentals in a Washington Kayak Club class. After that, I learned more from experienced paddlers who collectively had paddled what would eventually become the latest hot destinations of today. Those paddlers emphasized knowing what was going on out there and staying within one's ability. It's the same now, of course, but the approach then was to know a lot about your paddling environment and use fairly basic kayak skills. Planning was critical and hardly anyone could roll a sea kayak.

Today, most of the emphasis seems to be on equipment, kayak handling, and being good enough to overcome whatever you encounter. Many books on "all you need to know about sea kayaking" present very little beyond boat handling. That is fine if your goal is just to play with your kayak; but when you are exhausted, temporarily disabled with a muscle strain, or leading a group of confused paddlers, you need to know as much as possible about the seamanship side of the equation. That's because it is much easier to *stay* out of trouble than it is to *get* out of trouble.

I am now in the kayaking business, and have been for some time. I find that most paddlers do not set out to be "hot dog" boat handlers. They just want to be competent and safe as they explore the coast. Since they have varying degrees of ability, they often take a class and quickly find out what they can safely do with a kayak. Each person has a personal limit. It is not important what that limit is, only that the paddler stays within it. Once, at a meeting of instructors, I was criticized for not having a swim test for my students and for teaching a non-swimmer to kayak. Ironically, the critic was the one who sold my student her kayak.

There is nothing like teaching to help one learn. It has helped me analyze and improve my own technique; in fact, it forced me to do so. Often I've learned a new trick or two from my students. Uninhibited as they are, because of not knowing how to do it properly, they sometimes figure out how to do it better.

My favorite kayak navigation book is *Kayak Navigation* by David Burch. It has *everything* there is to know about navigation. But it is an encyclopedia, and best used as a reference, not a basic how-to book. In teaching, I have been unable to recommend a book that covers navigation the way I find myself doing it. After I had a few magazine articles published, Bob Koch of AlpenBooks Press asked me to write my own book on navigation. No problem, I thought, that's just a series of articles organized into a book.

Anyone who has seen me at a put-in knows of my limited organizational skills. Writing this book presented a dilemma a lot like loading my kayak. What do I include? What do I leave out? What is critical? And what is worth including just for fun? After thirty years of paddling, I'm still not certain about my gear selection, and I have no reason to expect that my selection of writing topics will be any more certain. Nevertheless, I believe this book has most of the information you will need to handle typical coastal kayaking situations.

I hope this book helps you sort out some ideas for paddling safely. I want to make navigation easier for you to understand so you have more fun with less risk. If you have some ideas on navigation, or comments on this book, I'd like to hear from you. You can write to me care of my publisher, AlpenBooks Press, or at Pacific Water Sports, 11011 Tukwilla International Boulevard, Tukwilla, WA 98168, or e-mail me at *Lee@pwskayaks.com*.

Pleasant Paddling,

Lee Moyer
February 2001

RIDDLE: What is it that when you guide a kayak trip, if your client doesn't have one he is more likely to give you one? And if you own this book, you are more likely to get one?

If you can't solve this riddle, e-mail me and I'll give you a tip.

Some boats are even more graceful than others. Photo courtesy Rippin' Productions—Jock Bradley

Acknowledgements

I appreciate the help of a lot of friends: Wolf Bauer, who taught me in the Washington Kayak Club class of 1969; Judy, my former paddling partner on most of my trips; Bob Morris, who took us on our first extended coastal trip; Ken and Angie Green, with whom I've shared most of my trips; David Burch, who wrote the most comprehensive kayak navigation book I've ever read; John Dowd, who wrote one of the first common-sense sea kayaking books; Ward Irwin, who shared his half century of paddling and editing experience; Dave Harrison, former owner of *Canoe & Kayak* magazine; Marge Mueller, who made a book from my ramblings; Rob Cookson, John Winskill, Steve Salins, Jock Bradley, and others who have helped with this book; and, of course, Experience, which is what one credits when he can't remember who shared the information with him.

Plan ahead to avoid disagreement. Photo courtesy Rippin' Productions—Jock Bradley

INTRODUCTION

*Safety is more dependent on your ability to
<u>control</u> your exposure to hazards than on
your ability to <u>handle</u> hazards.*

There is "traditional navigation" and what I call "good navigation." Traditional navigation takes into consideration such factors as distance, direction, boat speed, current and wind. With traditional navigation techniques borrowed from other, non-kayaking boaters, and with the appropriate tables and calculations, the kayaker can get a full evening's worth of dull math.

Good navigation, simply stated, is using the appropriate strategy to reach your destination easily and safely. Navigating a kayak in the real world is never boring. For the kayaker, good navigation replaces boredom and frustration with fun, You will have to consider the interest of island-hopping versus the freeway-like efficiency of a long direct crossing, and, because you will not be paddling alone, you will have to take into account the intangibles of your companions' capabilities and moods and the rights of dissenters who would prefer another route. To these you must add the restraints that seldom find their way into the texts. These might include bladder pressure, the right trolling speed for the fishing lure you are using, or the location of a good campsite.

Your navigation equipment can be simple. The only expensive items will be your charts, wristwatch, compass, and binoculars. Dividers and parallel rules are useful, but cheaper items will suffice. These are discussed in detail under Equipment in the Navigation Fundamentals chapter.

SAFETY IS WHAT IT'S ALL ABOUT

Why learn navigation? Because you want to paddle safely and competently. Being safe requires competence, but competence in several fields. Non-paddlers, novice paddlers, and some experienced paddlers judge kayaking ability solely by a person's boat-handling skills. In their minds, if you can roll, do a sculling brace, and sprint with the best of them, you are considered an expert. Becoming a good kayak handler is a legitimate goal, but its attainment does not necessarily mean one is a competent *touring* kayaker. One cannot take a track star and say he will be a good backpacker when he knows nothing of such things as hypothermia, map and compass use, keeping warm in adverse weather, and first aid. His leg strength will not compensate for his lack of knowledge of the other skills of backpacking.

Similarly, navigation skills complement kayak-handling skills. Your kayak-handling skills determine what conditions you are able to master. Your navigation skills usually determine what conditions you are subjected to. Safety is more dependent on your ability to *control your exposure to hazards* than on your ability to handle hazards. Good navigation will minimize your exposure to danger. Ultimately, your navigation skills are your greatest safety asset.

The keys to safe navigation:

1. Awareness of the kayaking environment
2. Good judgement
3. Avoiding unknown conditions
4. Advanced planning

5. Awareness of your own abilities and the abilities and psychology of your group

Safe kayak navigation requires not so much knowledge of geometry as an awareness of the kayaking environment: awareness of what nature is doing, the geography of the area, and the ability of your party. Good navigation includes group management skills, since members of the group need to know what is going on and need to be involved in making decisions. In addition to speed, direction and drift, navigation decisions must consider group psychology and ability.

Good judgment means avoiding unknown conditions as much as possible. You will want to know the weather, current and tidal conditions. You will want to know your own condition and ability, and the condition and ability of your partners. Avoid ignorance and carefully pick your knows.

Advance planning is what makes passive navigation possible.

While in the cockpit, good navigation is a passive activity, based on advanced planning, continuous observation and simple mental estimates. The cockpit is no place to be calculating, plotting, measuring, and handling your chart. You will just get your chart wet, frustrate the rest of the paddlers, and probably drop something overboard. You will also fall behind the group and frequently just waste time. While in the cockpit, good paddlers rarely do any calculating or plotting (navigational plotting, that is; mutinies are another matter).

Advance planning is what makes this passive navigation possible. Before you go into the water, you must learn as much as possible about the currents, weather, available facilities (be they sources of water or ice cream), geography, points of interest, landing and camping sites, alternative destinations, etc. Your planning will combine research, chart preparation, and something you already have—common sense.

As a navigator, you will need to monitor your group's capability. A good estimate of group speed is 3 knots. A day of 4-knot paddling is a day of fairly hard work. You will find it easier to paddle farther in a day by increasing your paddling time than by increasing your paddling effort. The key to keeping on schedule is to paddle consistently, rather than paddle hard and take rest breaks. Using 3 knots as your planned travel speed means you will have the energy to paddle a little harder when you need to compensate for navigational errors or potty breaks. In terms of miles per day, 10 is easy, 20 is a lot, and 30 is an athletic accomplishment (10 hours of paddling). To be safe, be conservative with your speed estimates.

Kayak navigation is often very simple. In calm conditions, if the chart shows the direction and distance to your destination, you simply point your craft in that direction and paddle that far. If you are following a shoreline, simply paddle along the beach to your destination. Even when navigation is not that simple, it needn't be very difficult. Adding in complicating factors just requires the skills you will learn in this book, along with a little practice.

TIP: Change leaders to keep everyone involved in navigating and decision making.

Navigation Fundamentals

In paddling an unfamiliar area, you need some source of clues.

Navigation requires that you be familiar with a few simple concepts Since the point of it all is to get somewhere safely and efficiently, you obviously need to know your starting point and destination. If you use a map and look out the window of your car for landmarks, you are already navigating—piloting, actually. You pilot your car as you drive to work, pilot yourself as you walk into the building and find your desk, and even pilot your fingers as they move on a keyboard, using the last letter as reference for the next letter. In known areas such as these, you don't even need to refer to a map or chart; you already know what to look for.

In paddling an unfamiliar area, you do need some source of clues. This is usually your chart, which shows a multitude of details and their locations. If you know your starting point, you know which way to go to your destination. If you want to go to Paradise Beach and can see on the chart that Paradise Beach is north of your starting point, you know you need to paddle north to get there. If you know your paddling speed, you can check the distance on the chart and estimate how long it will take to get there.

EQUIPMENT

Charts

The most important piece of navigational equipment is your chart. Charts are the maps of the marine world, but only landlubbers and jet skiers would call them "maps." Nautical types, the ultimate of whom are kayakers, call these maps charts.

Do not scrimp on charts. Get the best, even though they cost a lot of money. You may want a small-scale chart that shows a large area for overall planning, but for actual touring you will want your chart to show the finer details. Just identifying and locating a crucial camp-site not noticeable on a small-scale chart will make your investment in large-scale charts worthwhile. Paper charts are the norm, but electronic charts on CD are now available and are good because they allow you to print out a seamless chart of the area you want paddle, and to use any scale you want.

Nautical charts are available only through licensed dealers who must, by law, keep their stock up-to-date, discard out-of-date versions, and stay abreast of the latest notices to mariners. These charts are important legal documents; they were the first thing examined by attorneys when the Exxon Valdez piled onto the rocks. All other marine charts are unofficial civilian charts and are marked "Not for Navigation." That means they are not for navigation in conditions where life or financial fortunes depend on whether the chart has the latest notices to mariners and the most up-to-date versions of details, such as buoy light signals and navigation channel markers. For kayaking, a civilian guide or simplified version is often fine for navigation, even when it is labeled "Not for Navigation." Maybe the term should be "Not for Litigation."

You must protect your chart with a clear waterproof case. Buy a large case, because once you are on the water it is far easier to fold a large one with the chart inside than it is to continually open a smaller

The tools of navigation: Chart and (left to right, top to bottom) courser, dividers, altimeter, weather radio, marine compass, hiker's compass. Altimeters are useful for predicting weather by indicating changes in barometric pressure. A piece of paper, waterproof pen, watch, binoculars, and if desired, parallel rulers complete the gear.

one, pull out and refold the chart, and stuff it back inside without getting water inside. Use a double-sided clear case so you have twice the coverage and half the need to get into it while on the water. Waterproofing your chart is also wise (some come already waterproofed), but it is no substitute for a case.

Compass

The basic tool of the navigator is the magnetic **compass**; a gadget that indicates which way is north. There are two types of magnetic compasses: the **hiking compass** and the **marine compass**, which is usually deck mounted, although some hand-held models are available. Almost any type of compass will do, but your choice of compass will actually affect some of your navigation techniques. One mounted on your deck can't be left behind, works best for course maintenance, and is always handy. A hand-held hiking-type compass is convenient for taking ranges, identifying distant objectives and, of course, taking on an island hike. One of each is the best combination.

There are significant differences between hiking and marine compasses. Marine compasses read from the side, while hiking compasses read from above (some marine compasses can read from either the side or top, due to the optics of the domed lens). On a marine compass, the moving part that points north is a floating card with numbers on it that you read to determine direction. On a hiking compass, the needle moves and points at the numbers that are on the housing or bezel surrounding the moving needle.

Although a hiking compass is great for taking a bearing on some point off to the side as you paddle; overall, a marine compass is better. This deck-mounted compass is always handy and really hard to leave behind. It is also much easier to use for course keeping when you are doing a blind crossing and have to follow a compass course. That's because the flat hiking compass must be held level to get a reading. This interrupts the paddling cadence and discourages effective use of the compass.

The type of compass you use may determine what you use for reference directions, true or magnetic (see Navigation Terminology). A marine compass requires use of magnetic directions but some hiking compasses work well both ways. That's because many hiking compasses

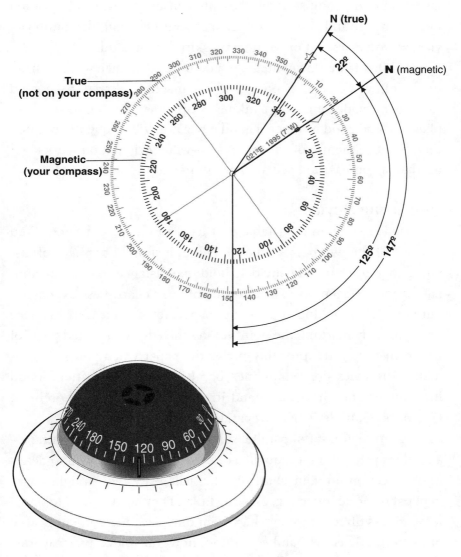

Figure 1. Compass rose (top) and marine compass

21

come with an adjustable declination scale— you merely "crank in" an area's declination to read true directions off the magnetic hiking compass. You can't do this with a marine compass. However, even with a hiking compass with a declination adjustment scale, it is still easier and less error-prone to use magnetic directions. If you have a favorite hiking compass you certainly can use it. Just keep it on a long string around your neck or tied to your Personal Floatation Device, so you can lay it on your spray skirt as you paddle.

While the marine compass is a definite advantage when you actually follow a compass course and use magnetic directions, a good case can be made for having a hiking compass as well. Yet, with proper planning and good weather, a good navigator will frequently use neither, because the use of continuous on-water orientation works better than a compass to keep a sense of direction.

Measuring Devices

Dividers are an adjustable tool used to measure distance. You put one of the two points on each end of a straight segment of distance on your chart. The dividers hold that distance so you can compare it to the legend or latitude scale of your chart. Less expensive, but not as cool looking, is a piece of paper. You can measure distance with paper by marking the points along the edge of a folded piece of paper. In fact, you'll probably prefer the paper when you start estimating distances along shorelines, because it will work better for odd little increments of distance and irregular routes along shorelines. (See page 38, under Chart Preparation.)

A protractor, set of parallel rulers, or clear plastic film with parallel lines printed on it, known as a courser, will work well to determine direction on your chart. Parallel rulers are two straight edges kept parallel by connecting, pivoting links. They are designed to transfer compass directions on a chart from one place to another. A piece of lined plastic is the handiest option, however folded paper works, although not quite as well as the protractor or parallel rulers. You'll also need a pencil for temporary navigation marks, and a ballpoint pen to add information to your chart.

TIP: If you don't have parallel rulers or lined plastic film to check a course, just roll a pen or pencil across your chart from the course line to the compass rose to get an approximate reading from the rose.

Watch

A wristwatch is essential because you need to know how long you have been paddling to estimate how far you have come. The most basic kind will be adequate. These days even the cheapest ones are waterproof, accurate, and hold up to clam digging.

Binoculars

A good pair of binoculars is important for navigation, since it aids in seeing your landmarks. Don't go for high power since it may have less field of view, be more vulnerable to motion, and require more ambient light. A pair of six-power binoculars will let you see more from a moving kayak than the eight-power version of the same model. Unfortunately, six-power will be harder to find because the manufacturers have determined that consumers want more power.

Weather Radio

A weather radio is very important in deciding whether to go out paddling. It is inexpensive and picks up the continuous weather channels almost everywhere along the coast. It is your best indicator of what the weather conditions will be like later. Usually it doesn't accurately indicate the conditions you are seeing, but it does give you a good idea of the trend, and that is what you need to know when deciding whether to launch. Will it get foggy, windy, or is a storm coming?

Adding It All Up

In reality, you have all the basic equipment you need if you have a compass, a chart, a folded sheet of paper, and a watch. The plastic film with lines on it is useful, but dividers and parallel rulers are not really necessary. Binoculars and a weather radio are good, especially if you are traveling some distance and might encounter questionable weather, but for short trips they are not essential. Chapter 2, Chart Preparation, tells you how to put all these to work for you.

NAVIGATION TERMINOLOGY

The purpose of the compass directions is usually course reference, not course maintenance.

Direction

The most important navigation detail is direction. The direction to a destination point is called the bearing of that point. The usual way to define a direction is in degrees, measured clockwise from north, which is defined as 0 degrees. Thus, east is 90 degrees, south 180 degrees and west 270 degrees. In describing NSEW (north, south, east, or west) the names are fine, but on intermediate directions, degrees are much simpler. Most people can figure out 22 degrees much easier than north-northeast.[1] When you start considering corrections for drift or magnetic variation, which we will cover later, degrees are the only way to go.

Direction is often the most confusing detail. The problem is that there are two basic sets of directions. True directions are how the mapmaker sees the world; magnetic directions are how your

---

[1]Northeast is half way between north and east. North northeast is halfway between north and northeast. See, degrees is a simpler way of saying it!

compass sees the world. The standard you are probably most familiar with is true, where north is at the top of the world. The pivot axis of a globe extends through the north and, of course, south poles. This system is universal on maps and charts and is the best one for some navigation, such as driving a car. But kayakers, like hikers, use a magnetic compass and some of us can't paddle and think at the same time. That's why you need to get comfortable with magnetic directions.

By definition, your compass is magnetic and points toward the magnetic north pole, which is somewhere between Hudson Bay and the true north pole. If you are located due south of Hudson Bay, e. g., along the Mississippi valley of the United States, the true north pole and magnetic north pole are pretty much in the same direction and you can just use your compass and call it true north. However, in most of the world, including the rest of the U.S. and Canada, your compass doesn't point toward true north. For example, in British Columbia it points to the right, east of true north, and in Maine it points left, west of true north. And up in grizzly country it might point straight at that shotgun just under your deck—don't forget you are using a magnetic compass.

Declination

The difference between magnetic north and true north is called variation (or more often, declination). In western North America, declination is how far clockwise your compass points from true north. For example, on the kayakers' Mecca of Canada's west coast, the variation is in the 20-degree range, way too much to ignore. Thus, if your destination is to be in a certain direction on the chart (remember, chart=true north), just subtract the declination from that bearing to get the magnetic bearing you want on your compass (you are converting chart to compass, true to magnetic). Or, if your direction is to be in a certain direction on the compass (compass=magnetic north), just add the declination to see the true direction you'll want to go on your chart (you are converting compass to chart, magnetic to true). Keep in mind that in eastern North America, declination is how far counter-clockwise your compass points from true north, and all the corrections mentioned above need to be reversed. Too confusing? That's why we do all the thinking at home and not in the cockpit.

To figure it out yourself, just try a few examples. Assume you're on the west coast. Your compass says you are looking at 125 degrees and the chart shows a variation of 22 degrees E. You are looking at 147 degrees true on the chart. To get the compass direction when you want to paddle at 205 degrees on the chart, subtract the 22 degrees to get the magnetic direction of 183 degrees, which you read directly on the compass. To avoid confusion in the field[2] do the math at home, mark it on your chart (more on this later), and use magnetic compass readings as you paddle. (See figure 1.)

Deviation is the deflection of your compass due to a local magnetic field, such as a steel camp stove stored just below your compass, or those great 100-watt speakers on your deck. Oops, I forgot, you are not a power boater. But do pay attention to ferrous metal objects you store near your compass. This is more of a problem if your compass is mounted far forward over your bow storage area, where you are likely to put your axe or canned beans.

The compass rose (circle) on your chart makes the magnetic versus true direction easy to understand. Both of these systems are shown together as concentric rings with the directions printed on them. The inner ring is magnetic, the outer true, and the declination is written in the rose. You can compare a direction with the rose and read magnetic or true directly off the chart without the high math of addition and subtraction. You just have to use the correct ring.

---

[2]Paddling in fields is popular in Nebraska, where navigation usually consists of learning the farmer's irrigation schedule.

The purpose of the compass is usually course reference, not course maintenance. Remember those old war movies with the scene on the bridge of the ship? Who is the highest-ranking person and what is he doing? He is the captain and he's looking out the window. Who is the lowest ranking person and what is he doing? He is the steersman and he's watching the compass. Why? Because continuously watching the compass makes you seasick. You want to be the captain and look out the window. Whenever possible, maintain your course by watching the sun, wind, waves and other outside features (more on this later, too). Check your compass once in a while to be sure all is OK. If you must paddle in waves and stare at your compass, don't bother with a meal before hand or, if you do eat, be sure to wear a spray skirt.

Distance

The globe you used back in school suggests the logical unit of distance measurement—the nautical mile (NM). All your life you've used the statute mile, the one on your car odometer. The nautical mile is approximately $1\frac{1}{7}$ statute miles. The really neat thing about the nautical mile is that it is derived from the lines on your globe. A nautical mile is 1 minute of latitude. Since there are 60 minutes in a degree, moving north and south 1 degree in latitude is moving 60 nautical miles. These same lines are on your chart. In fact, there are 5-minute or 10-minute latitude lines across your chart everywhere. You always have this 5 or 10 NM reference, no matter how you fold the chart. Best of all, the chart borders (typically the left and right ones) are latitude scales marked off in minutes and tenths of minutes, giving you great nautical-mile legends to compare map points to for a quick and accurate estimation of distances.

If you look at a globe again, you'll see all the latitude lines are equidistant. No matter where you are in the world, your chart has this handy latitude reference. Now look at the longitude lines. They go north and south and meet at the poles. Note that they are not the same distance apart as you go north and south, so take care not to use the longitude scale chart borders (typically the top and bottom borders) to estimate distance.

Speed

The obvious unit to use for speed is a nautical mile per hour, which is called a knot. Going 3 knots is going 3 nautical miles per hour, about 3½ statute miles per hour. This is a very typical group speed and a good estimate for group touring. Since drag on a kayak doubles with an increase of 1 knot, to travel at 4 knots means you will put out twice as much energy per mile. This has a very equalizing effect on fast paddlers versus slower ones. By the way, unless you are truly talking about very slow acceleration, please do not say "knots per hour," which would be saying "nautical miles per hour per hour" and make you sound like a landlubber.

CHARTS—PUTTING THEM TO WORK

You can get started understanding charts with just a few basics.

Charts show an amazing amount of detail, more than just what direction and distance it is to some place. They indicate small rocks just breaking the surface, the type of beach at your landing site, the shoal areas, river mouths, points, inlets, cliffs, water depth, type of bottom, visual features for navigation, shoreline topography, access possibilities, and literally any other detail significant for navigation. However, you have to keep in mind for whom the charts are intended. Most navigational information sources, such as charts, current and tide tables, The Coastal Pilot or Sailing Directions, and similar information, come from government agencies and are intended for, but not restricted to, commercial and military users.

These government sources are quite accurate; however, small details of interest to kayakers that are of little value to commercial navigation, may not be up-to-date. For instance, along the British Columbia coast and the Inside Passage there is little information about currents, except for points that are actually on the commercial route. Changes in small topographical details, which are important to paddlers, are infrequent, of course, but are even less frequently updated on the charts.

Although the accuracy and detail of official charts is impressive, winter storm deposition and erosion, geologic rebound from receding glaciers, river flood deposition and erosion, slides and other natural or man-caused occurrences can affect the shallow water depths quite easily. You should not bet on something being passable just because the chart says it is.

Your best guide to interpreting information included on U. S. charts is the U. S. Government's *Chart No. 1*, which is not a chart at all, but an inexpensive booklet of symbols. There are commercial versions as well. *Chart No. 1* gives a complete legend of symbols and terminology, and is easy to read. If you just read through it lightly, you will pick up the general concepts of symbols and terminology. You can look up specific details later as you need to. Canadian charts are very similar to U.S. charts, but they use a different low tide datum and Canadian charts are going to metric units. For obvious reasons, other charts around the world seem to be very similar, too. If you are comfortable reading U. S. charts, you should have little problem with charts from most other sources. So just study *Chart No.1* to learn the symbols you think you will need.

You can get started understanding charts with just a few basics. Chart terminology is important. Tide refers to the height of the water surface: rising, falling, high, low, etc. Mean lower low water (MLLW) is the average level of the lowest tide of each day (not each cycle) and is the datum or 0 (zero) height on U. S. charts. Because Canada uses a significantly lower datum, Canadian tables list far fewer minus tides, and all levels are labeled as higher than the U.S. standard would label them. Whether you are in Canada, or the U.S., this difference in datums doesn't really affect navigation, since obstacles and depths are measured from the same reference on any given chart. Each chart has printed information telling you the datum from which all depths are measured.

Those charted water depths and feature heights that affect hull clearance are measured from the datum level. A minus tide means a water level below this datum. For example, a level 3 feet below this datum is a −3-foot tide. Another example is, at a tide height of 6 feet, anything that reached less than 6 feet above the datum is underwater. Features that reach higher than 6 feet will protrude above the water by their height, minus 6 feet. Therefore, a rock marked as 9 feet high will stick up out of the water 3 feet, and on a tide of -3 feet, that rock will stick up 12 feet. (See figure 2.)

Charted land-height features useful for navigation are measured from the high water mark or coastline. The high water mark varies considerably, and is usually not defined on the chart. It is well below the normal vegetation line. As you sit in your kayak ready to take a picture of the Statue of Liberty, wait for low tide so it will look more impressive at 6 or 8 feet higher than its official height of 460 feet.

Those numbers and marks shown all over the water areas on your chart generally indicate depth. In deep-water areas, the depth is measured in fathoms (1 fathom=6 feet). In shallower areas, it is in fathoms and fractions of a fathom, or fathoms and feet (e.g. 33 feet would be printed as $5\frac{1}{2}$ fathoms or 5_3). A cross or plus sign (+) indicates an obstruction that is covered by water at a 0 tide height. An asterisk (*) represents an obstruction that is exposed at a 0 tide height. A number by one of these last two symbols will indicate how much water covers a + or how far out of the water an * stands at a 0 tide height. Wiggly-branched lines indicate kelp beds. Short abbreviations or symbols on the water usually indicate type of bottom: s for sand, rky for rocky, m for mud.

Numbers shown on the land areas are usually altitude. Very small islands that seem to be assigned numbers are not numbered at all. Their number shows the altitude of the highest point on the island. Mountains and hills that seem to be distinct when viewed from the water will have their altitudes indicated as well. There are also contour lines that indicate the topography of the land surface that is visible from the water. This helps you identify coastline by showing you what a ridgeline or valley looks like. (See figure 3.)

An easy feature to learn is color, although its meaning sometimes varies. Land is gold or gray, deep water is white. Water that is less than 10 fathoms (60 feet) or 10 meters (if metric units) is shaded light blue, and land that is covered by high tide, but exposed by a 0 tide, is

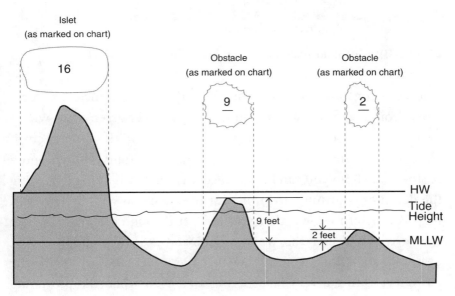

Figure 2. Datum (zero height), charted water depth, and feature height

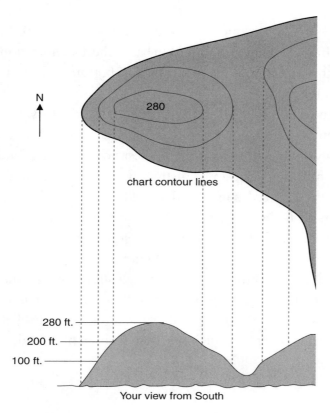

Figure 3. Land contour lines, and what they mean at water level

colored green or olive drab. Since depths and clearances are measured from mean low water, you can paddle over green areas whenever there is a positive tide height. But if you think you can cut it close and depend on complete accuracy, take along a lunch and a partner on whom you can blame the occasional grounding. Knowing the depth of your intended route for the time you will be there will help you determine whether you can get through a passage, where the current will increase, or where the waves will be choppier. For example, a shallow area will steepen the waves and accelerate the current, creating a very challenging area even when the prevailing weather and paddling conditions are favorable.

Charts — Putting Them to Work

It may seem like a chart has a lot of confusing data, but there is one thing to remember: if there is a large mass of confusing symbols in an area, it is probably a very interesting place to paddle. After all, it's not the water, but the shoreline and bottom that make sea kayaking so interesting.

Breaking trail with a kayak in Alaska. Photo by Lee Moyer

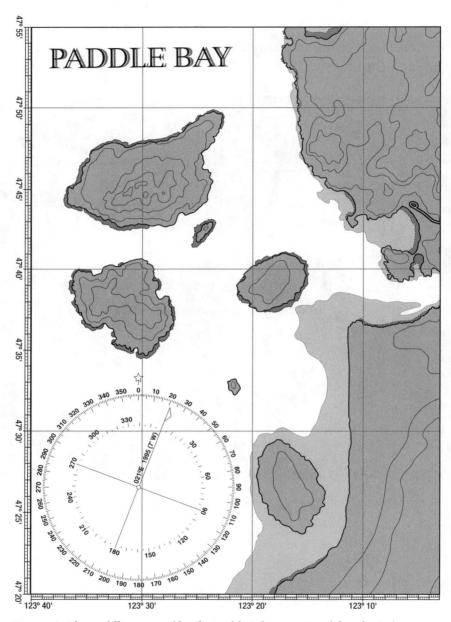

Figure 4. The paddling area (depths and heights ommitted for clarity)

Chapter 2

CHART
PREPARATION

Remember to check with area clubs and paddling friends, because they constitute the best overall intelligence.

The easiest place to prepare for your navigating is at home, not piecemeal while on the water. At home you can study the area in which you want to paddle and prepare the charts so you can paddle and navigate passively, by observation, not calculation.

We will use the "Paddle Bay" chart, figure 4 as the basis for the discussion of chart preparation.

POINTS OF INTEREST

First, you will mark on your brand new Paddle Bay chart all significant points of interest, such as the launch site, the ends of crossings, potential camp and break sites, alternate landing sites and take outs, and facilities along the way that might be useful. (See figure 5 to see how this information is noted.) Don't forget the private spot no one else could possibly know about that you saw in a magazine's list of "Ten Best Secret Kayak Sites." And remember to check with area clubs and paddling friends, because they constitute the best overall intelligence for the important information that kayakers need.

CROSSINGS

Next, study the area you will explore and mark with straight lines all strategic crossings on the chart (also on figure 5). Do not limit this to the probable route you intend to take. Instead, connect land points, launch and campsites, and all other strategic points of interest that could be involved in crossings, whether you plan to go there or not. Even if you don't make these specific crossings, if you modify your route while under way these lines will become useful bits of information to help you estimate legs of the route you do choose. If you are just planning a day trip, you probably know your start, the route and destination, and what the weather will be. You just go out and paddle the route. However, on a longer trip you should build in more flexibility because at some point you probably will deviate significantly from your initial plans. In fact, some of your best trips will just be covering an area with a very loose schedule of where to be when, or no schedule at all. Your charts will then have a lot of information on which to base decisions as you wander about.

Now, measure the distance of each crossing. To do this, take a large piece of paper folded to get a long straightedge, and lay the folded edge along the line of each route. Mark the ends of a crossing on the paper and compare it to the latitude edge of your chart to get the length of the crossing. (See figure 6 for how to do this.) Of course, you can use those neat dividers for this as well, but paper is cheaper. To use dividers, spread the legs to span the crossing. Compare this

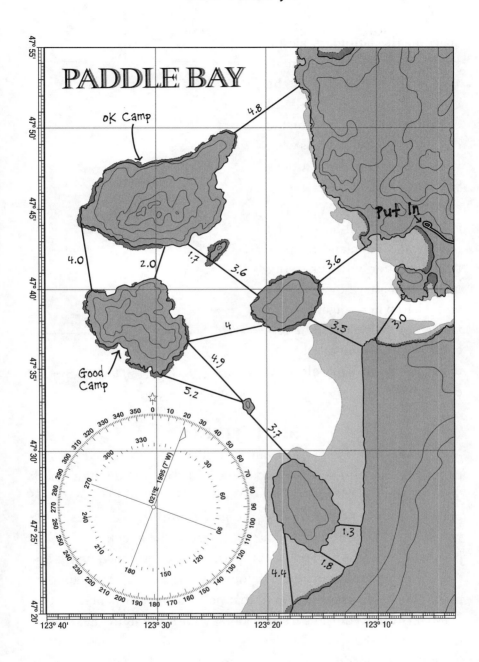

Figure 5. The paddling area with notes and crossings added

space to the latitude scale on the border to get the distance.

Write the lengths of the crossings along the middle of each of the crossing lines on the chart. Figure 6 now shows what your chart would look like once you have marked the crossings and their distances. When you are done, you will have all the islands and mainland features tied together with crossing lines. No matter how you fold your chart when you are on the water, you will have some references with which to estimate distances. Soon you will have even more.

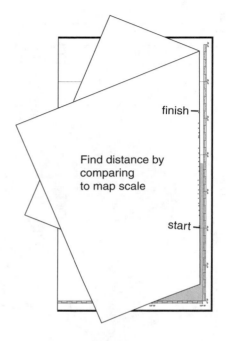

finish

Find distance by comparing to map scale

start

Figure 6. Use a piece of folded paper to measure crossing distances.

SHORELINES

To measure shoreline distances, again use your folded piece of paper. Mark a point near one end of the folded edge and put the mark over the start of the first leg of your route. Hold it in place with the point of your pencil and rotate the paper until the edge lies along your route. Without moving the paper, move the pencil to a farther point along your route and hold the paper with the pencil point. Rotate the paper around the pencil point so it again lies across another point along your route and hold that point with your pencil. In this manner, "walk" your folded edge along your route to the next destination. Mark that point on your folded edge. It is not necessary to mark the intermediate points; they are simply pivot points for your pencil as you proceed down the route. Just mark the start and end points clearly. You are estimating an irregular total distance by aggregating a bunch of short straight distances. Now, take the folded edge and once again compare it to the latitude scale on the side of your chart to get the distance in nautical miles. Draw a line on your chart on either land or water, connecting the start and finish, and mark it with the distance. You are measuring the route you would take if you were in a hurry and minimizing the distance: going from one point of land to the next, following the shore closely around protruding curves of land, cutting across small bays. Use this technique to mark all shoreline trip segments so you can estimate the length of any part of your trip by adding up the segments (fig. 8).

If there are islands in the area of your trip, measure the distance around each one by "walking" your folded paper around the islands, too (fig. 7). Be careful to note the start point (which, in the case of islands, is also the end point), because it's easy to lose track of where you began. Write the circumferences of the islands on the islands, and circle these numbers so they are easy to find. The circles will remind you that the numbers refer to the islands' circumferences. Although you won't be paddling around all the islands, it is easy to estimate a distance along one island's shore by simply estimating what part of the circumference you intend to paddle. Suppose you intend to cross to an island and paddle along its shore to a campsite. It is easy to estimate that you will paddle about one-fourth of the way around the island, so that distance is one-fourth of the measured circumference you marked on the chart.

Now let's see what we have. Looking at figure 8, assume you want to paddle from the put-in to "Good Camp." You will paddle 3.2 miles along the shore to a point, then 3.6 miles on the first crossing, 6 miles along the first island (slightly less than half the island's circumference), 4 miles on the second crossing, 6.5 miles along the second island (not quite one-third of the circumference). This adds up to a total of 23.3 miles. That's a long but do-able day. Fine accuracy

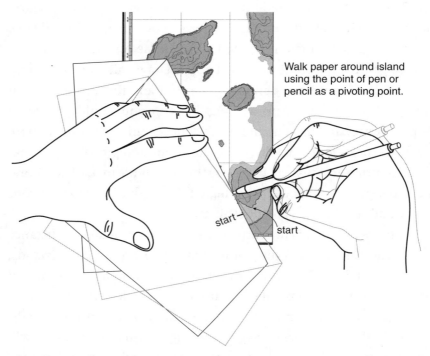

Walk paper around island using the point of pen or pencil as a pivoting point.

start

start

Figure 7. The folded piece of paper can be "walked" around islands or other irregular areas to measure distances.

isn't important for most decisions; you just want to decide strategic stops for such things as lunch and camp.

DIRECTIONS

Following a shoreline requires no compass work at all. However, on a crossing a compass will confirm your direction where visual clues will not. You already have your crossings marked (fig. 8), but now you need the bearing (the direction toward the destination) you would use in going along a route. Again, you use your trusty sheet of folded paper. Lay the chart flat and locate the nearest compass rose. Lay the folded edge along the crossing and then carefully, without rotating the paper, slide it until the straight edge goes exactly

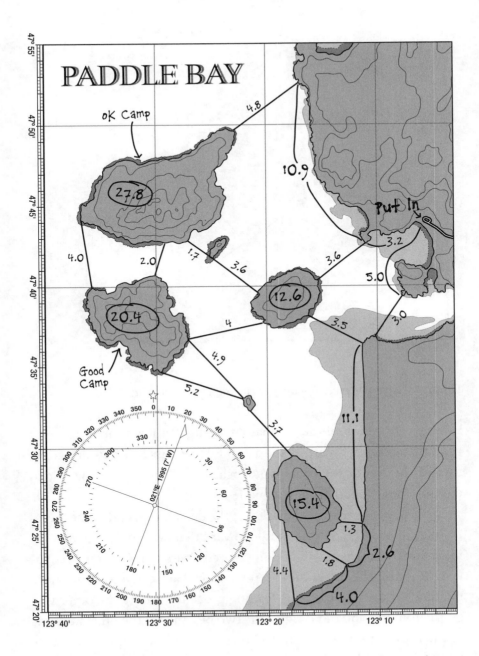

Figure 8. The paddling area with shoreline distances and island circumferences added

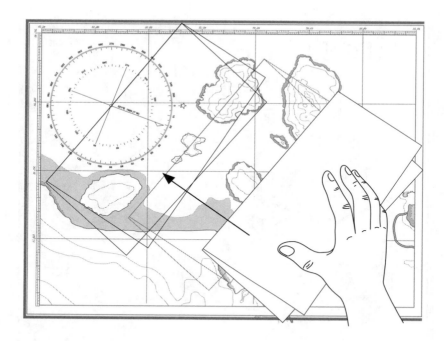

Figure 9. Using one piece of paper to calculate route bearing

through the center of the compass rose (fig. 9). Read the bearing off the inner magnetic part of the rose. For example, if you are going toward the top of the chart, your bearing will be where the folded edge crosses the top of the magnetic rose.

Read that bearing and mark it at the destination end of the crossing (see figure 11). As you paddle toward that destination, that is the magnetic bearing you will use on your compass to note your destination. It is also the direction you point your kayak if you do not have to allow for drift. Repeat this reading procedure going the other way on the route. If you did it right, the two bearings at the opposite ends of the route should differ by 180 degrees. With a couple of practice tries, you should be able to maintain accuracy within a few degrees, which is close enough for most kayak navigation. If you use parallel

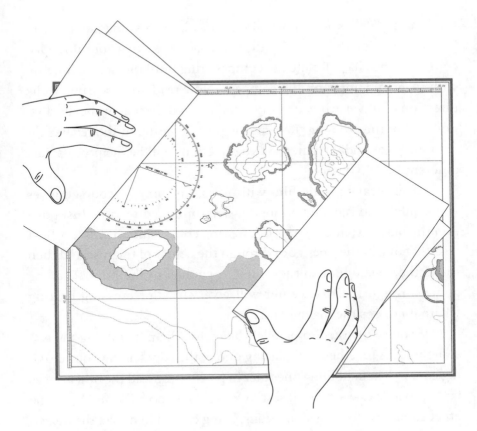

Figure 10. Using two pieces of paper to calculate route bearing

rulers or a clear piece of film with parallel lines on it, you can be within a degree.

You can improve your accuracy by using two folded sheets of paper. Lay one along your crossing. Lay the other through the center of the compass rose and rotate it until it is parallel to the first piece of paper (fig. 10). You can probably "eyeball" this parallelism to within a couple of degrees.

Another way to determine the bearings on the chart is by using your hiking compass. Just align the straight edge of your compass on the compass rose along the magnetic north/south. Rotate the chart until the needle of the compass lines up with the rose magnetic north. Without moving the chart, lay the compass edge along your intended course on the chart. Rotate the compass ring until the needle lines up with magnetic north on the compass. Now read your bearing at the direction of travel arrow on your compass and mark it at the destination end of the crossing. Repeat this process going in the reverse direction. If you did it right, the two directions will be reciprocals; i.e., different by 180 degrees.

Clear, heavy plastic film with lines, known as a courser, gives you a quick and accurate option for determining direction. Just position the plastic so it covers your crossing course and the rose. Adjust it so that one of the lines goes through the center of the rose and then rotate the plastic film so the course is parallel to the lines. The line going through the rose center will give you your crossing bearing where it crosses the magnetic scale.

If you've invested in parallel rulers, use them by folding the two straightedges together, and placing one of the edges along your crossing course. Then, holding one ruler in position, spread the other out as far as possible toward the closest rose. Hold it in position and bring the other ruler next to it. By this means, being careful to not let the instrument slide, walk the rulers across the chart until one of the rulers crosses the center of the rose and gives you your crossing bearing.

READY TO GO

Congratulations! Your chart is now fully prepared (fig. 11). It has all the significant features of the area noted. It has strategic distances along shorelines, along crossings and around islands. It also has the magnetic bearings of all the possible crossings. Now put it in a waterproof chart case and it is ready to use.

You will want to keep your chart dry, so be careful how you put it in the chart case, because you don't want to have to open the case as you paddle off the edge of the world. Lay the case over your chart and

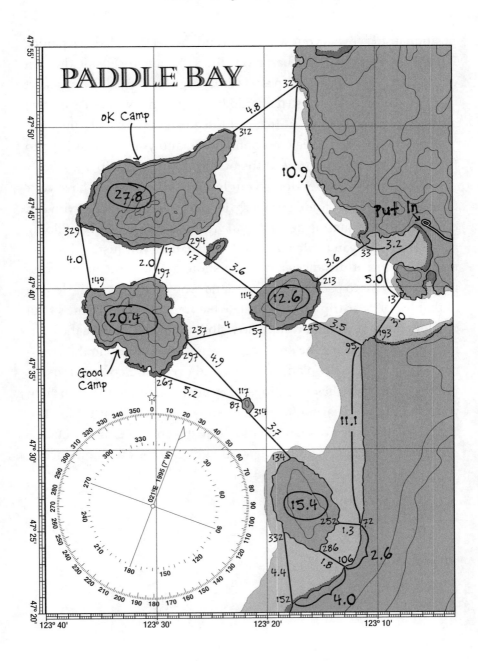

Figure 11. The paddling area with crossing bearings added, and ready to go.

position it so it covers your whole area and the nearby reference points, if possible. Then fold the chart along lines that are just inside the area of the chart case. If your map area is too large for this, and your chart case is clear on both sides (it should be), you can lay the case on two adjacent areas of your chart to cover the greater entire paddling area. Your final fold will be the common border, and you will just have to flip the chart case over to read the other part of your trip.

Here's the payoff for doing your homework: when you have your fully-prepared chart folded properly in your waterproof case, you can easily do any estimating needed to navigate your route without doing any serious on-water calculations. For distance, you just add up the marked segment distances along the shore and any included crossing. If you want to paddle along an island, you can estimate the length of that leg of your trip by estimating what fraction of the island's total circumference you will travel. If the visibility is bad, you have the bearings and distances for the crossings. Even if you cannot do the crossing you had originally planned to do, and even if no compass rose is visible, your chart has directions of nearby crossings that can help you estimate the bearing for the crossing you now want to do. The rest of what is called basic navigation is just techniques and tricks for using this information, and judgment, which comes with practice.

NAVIGATING SHORELINES

*In the real world there are seldom days that
are calm.*

Kayak touring is typically done along the shoreline. This is great, because that is where you see the most marine life, the sea bottom, and the interesting bottom critters. In addition, the nearby land has scenery, wildlife, and points of interest. Navigation along the shoreline is usually easy, because bigger boat traffic cannot get that close, and potty stops will be closer and will require less creativity. Your ability to read charts, along with your navigation skills, will enable you to predict water conditions along the shore, help you locate hazards, and make your shoreline exploring safer and more fun.

SURF AND WAVES

In mellow conditions, paddling along a shoreline is easy. You only have to stay far enough offshore to be out of the breaking surf and to avoid hitting obstacles in shallow water. This is a magical place to enjoy watching all the crawling, swimming, paddling and flying creatures. Nowhere else is there such diversity of critters. If you don't think so, just take a look at the critters paddling with you.

Along a typical beach you have the waves breaking harmlessly onto it and, in all probability, you'll have a safe landing. You just paddle your kayak onto the beach and get out. Hit the beach at an angle so you can slide onto it easily and do less damage to your kayak. In calm conditions, you can even land parallel to the beach to be most gentle to your kayak. The greatest hazard may be the landowner's dog or getting mud on your feet.

However, in the real world there are seldom days that calm. Waves of some sort are usually encountered in any landing. And as waves grow, your once-easy landing becomes a surf landing.

Surf is a four-letter word that means, "Gosh, those are big waves hitting that beach!" And the surf doesn't have to be particularly big. Size is relative to your skill; so don't be fooled by the actual size of the waves. Even small waves mean you will have to pay attention to what they are doing and know how to handle your kayak in those conditions.

> **CAUTION!** Beware of stepping out on the shore side of the kayak when there are waves coming in. You could easily suffer a broken ankle as the next wave slides your heavily loaded kayak into your firmly-planted foot.

WHAT ARE THESE THINGS CALLED WAVES?

The orbital wave theory explains why a kayak often broaches in a following sea

First, let's talk about the waves themselves. A wave is an oscillation moving across the surface of the water. After a wave passes a point on the water, the water looks pretty much as it did before, but

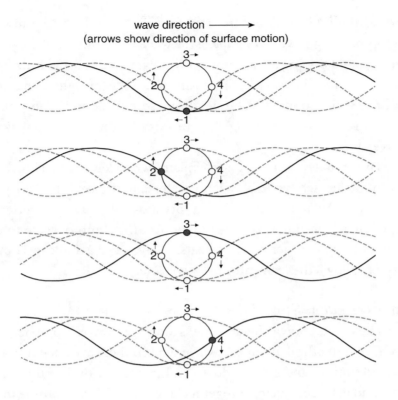

Figure 12. A cup floating in the water: orbital wave theory

as the wave went by some interesting things happened. Look at figure 12; if you were a Styrofoam cup floating in the trough of a wave, as a wave approaches you would be drawn toward the wave, as shown in position 1. As the wave moves under you, you would rise, (position 2). At the crest, you would be moving with the wave (position 3). Finally, as the wave goes by, you will drop down toward the trough (position 4), returning to the trough (position 1), and starting the cycle all over again. Viewed from the side as the wave passes, you would have moved in a circle. This is the orbital wave theory.

This oscillation motion has a significant effect on kayak handling. As the wave approaches, your kayak will be drawn toward it. If you are parallel to the wave, this motion toward the on-coming crest tends to pull the kayak out from under you if you don't lean toward the approaching wave. The slope of the wave will compound the problem. To avoid tipping over, follow the fundamental rule of kayak handling: lean into the wave. At first this doesn't seem right or natural, but once you've done it a couple of times it will soon become automatic. It is very similar to edging your skis into the hill when making a traverse.

The orbital wave theory also explains why a kayak often broaches in a following sea: your bow is in water moving back toward you, your stern is in water pushing you forward— if you aren't perfectly perpendicular to the wave, it will tend to turn you broadside to the wave. But unlike other types of boats, a kayak can avoid capsizing if its pilot follows the lean-into-the-wave rule.

Waves+Beach=Surf

The orbital wave theory breaks down as waves approach the beach. At a depth of about one wave length, the waves begin to feel the land bottom and start to do several important things: they slow down and get steeper, closer together, and taller. They continue to do this as the water gets shallower, until they get so steep they become unstable and break. At this point they are called surf. Waves break in shallow water— water that is only about $1^1/2$ times as deep as a wave is high. Thus 2-foot waves will break in 3 feet of water. Typical of shallow-sloped sand beaches, this classic surf condition is called spilling surf (no, it is not named after what is happening to the paddler who is experiencing it). The other type of surf is dumping surf (I know what you are thinking!) Dumping surf is a steep-beach action, where the waves break directly onto the beach. Advanced kayak skills are required to land safely on dumping surf.

> **CAUTION!** Capsizing in a surf landing risks more than a soaking. Because of the shallow water, serious cervical spine injuries can result if you are not skilled in kayak surfing techniques.

Waves and Weather

There are two types of weather-caused waves: wind waves and swells. Wind waves are caused by the weather you are currently experiencing. With a lot of wind you get large waves. With more fetch (the distance upwind to land), you get even larger waves. If the wind has been blowing for a long time, you also get larger waves. The more times you tell the story and the fewer the actual number of witnesses, the larger the waves get. However, as the wind dies (yours or nature's), the waves die and it gets calm. These wind-caused waves are the ones you get on inland water and on the open coast.

Sometimes you can avoid the conditions that cause stronger wind and bigger waves. The longer the fetch, the larger the waves will be. The longer the wind has been blowing, the larger the waves. You can be in a quick squall with fierce winds but not experience much in the way of waves for a short while. Typically, winds freshen in the afternoon; so paddling earlier in the day should result in easier paddling conditions. This is especially true in good weather, when the sun warms the landmass. This warms the air, causing it to rise, and allows strong onshore winds of cooler air to replace it.

Swells, on the other hand, are open coast waves caused by other weather systems, perhaps far distant from where you are paddling. There could be a low-pressure front 200 miles north that is sending 6-foot seas to your area. They will be very uniform, long, and fast. They are predictable by forecasters. Another low to the south may be sending 5-foot seas. Because of these size differences, their velocities and frequencies will be different. If the 5-footer and the 6-footer arrive together, you might experience an 8-foot wave. When the crest of one arrives with the trough of the other, they cancel each other and the sea might be hardly noticeable. This regular pattern is why waves on a coastal beach get bigger and smaller in a somewhat predictable cycle. This is sometimes called phasing, as when the waves from different sources arrive in phase or out of phase.

If you count waves, you will see that there is a regular cycle of growing and diminishing waves. For example, if you count twenty waves, starting with what seems to be the biggest wave, you may find that number twelve, for example, is also a biggest wave. Try it again and soon you will see the phase pattern. You can use that pattern for your landing. Be careful: if you forget that bigger waves will break in deeper water, and you paddle up to where the waves are starting to break and then start your count, you may hear the next wave before you see it.

To land in spilling surf, approach shore slowly and note how the break-line moves in and out with the size of the waves. Once you recognize the phase pattern and the in-and-out range of the break-line, the actual landing is pretty easy. Sit just outside the break-line of the largest wave. Once it breaks, watch carefully. Let the next wave go under you and, if it broke closer to shore (it should have, if you counted correctly), paddle toward its break-line. Then watch the next wave, which will be smaller, and after it breaks paddle up to its break-line. Repeat this process until you approach half of what you counted as the cycle of waves (number six out of the twelve in our example). That means you are at the smallest part of the cycle. When the next wave breaks, chase it all the way to shore.

In moderate surf, this technique will probably get you to shore without actually surfing. Once there, get out, secure your paddle and grab your bowline. With all your adrenaline assisting, you now could frantically drag your loaded kayak up the beach, just ahead of the reach of the breaking waves. But why work so hard? Let the water do the work for you. The larger waves that break farther offshore also wash farther up the shore. You landed at the low point in the cycle, so now each wave completing the cycle will flow farther up the beach. If you wait a bit after getting out of your kayak, each time a larger wave washes farther up the shore it will float your kayak just a little bit farther, too. Just enough for you to easily pull it a bit more up the beach. Once the cycle is complete, you will actually have to muscle it a little farther or tie it off so it can't escape, but most of the heavy work was done for you. Now you will be ready to help the others or unload your boat.

> **CAUTION!** These navigation tactics make surf landing easier and safer, but you still need to know enough about boat handling to know how to lean into the waves, brace, and side-surf onto a broach landing. Usually a mistake made in a surf landing just means you and your gear wash up on the shore rather ingloriously, but don't underestimate the hazard. Dumping, even in shallow surf, can easily result in serious cervical spine injury.

If you are landing in waves of about 1½ feet or less, you don't have to surf at all. Just approach the beach slowly and watch behind you. As a breaking wave approaches, do a hard backstroke to anchor your kayak, and allow the wave to slip under you. You may get wet as you are hit in the back by the wave, but you probably won't be otherwise affected. Just continue toward shore, repeating the backstroke to keep the succeeding waves from carrying you too fast, and starting you surfing.

> **TIP:** Keep a notepad in your shirt pocket or deck bag to note points of interest as you paddle. At the end of the day, when you are somewhere dry, add the notes to your chart.

Waves and Topography

As you paddle offshore, watch your chart for reefs, and remember the phasing effect of open-water seas. It is common for a reef to be deep enough underwater that most waves will cross it without breaking, but the largest waves in the phase cycle can overcome this depth, feel the reef, and break as they move across it. As you paddle open areas, watch for those occasional breaking waves. If they seem to happen in the same place, they could be a warning of a shallow, dangerous reef. Also watch for foam patches. These are often the result of breaking waves at an open-water reef. Check upwind of them for breaking waves.

Because of the shallow-water effects listed above, the underwater topography will have a major effect on the surface conditions in which you paddle. Shallow areas cause wave refraction. As a straight wave comes in from offshore to a curved beach, the parts of the wave that first encounter a shallow area will slow down. Meanwhile, the portion of the wave that hasn't yet encountered a shallow area will continue on in at full speed. This wave refraction will cause the wave to turn into shallow areas, e.g., the curved end of a beach toward a headland, the slowest parts turning the most. This turning (refraction) causes those portions of the wave in the shallow, curved areas to spread across a wider section of beach. Slower water over a wider beach results in less wave energy per lineal foot of beach, and thus smaller surf. That is why the easiest surf landing sites are usually at the ends of beaches. See figure 13 and especially Protection Head in figure 14 for illustrations of wave refraction.

Wave refraction will cause the opposite effect on a point. If the point is shallow offshore, i.e., not a cliff going directly into the water, the wave will tend to wrap around the point and focus its energy on the point. See Oshytte Point in figure 14 for an illustration of this phenomenon. You will have the combined effect of concentrated energy and shallow water making water at the point much rougher than that in nearby areas. If you are following the shoreline, be very careful about rounding a point. It may be best to follow the shoreline toward the point to check for a landing site, but in strong wave conditions you should head well offshore before rounding the point. Points have interesting effects on current as well, as you will see later in Making the Point (page 61).

If there is a small islet within the surf zone, be very cautious about going between it and the shore (see Deception Island in figure 14). There will be a shallow area between the islet and the shore that causes the waves on both sides of the islet to turn into that area.

These waves will be smaller than those nearby, but because they will be coming from two directions, these waves (called interfering waves) cause a very difficult paddling environment. Landing at such an area behind an island often seems the safe thing to do, but in this case it can be very dangerous.

Conversely, as the tide recedes and the islet becomes connected to the shore, this area will be a great place to land, because it forces the surf to turn radically and dissipate energy (compare Protection

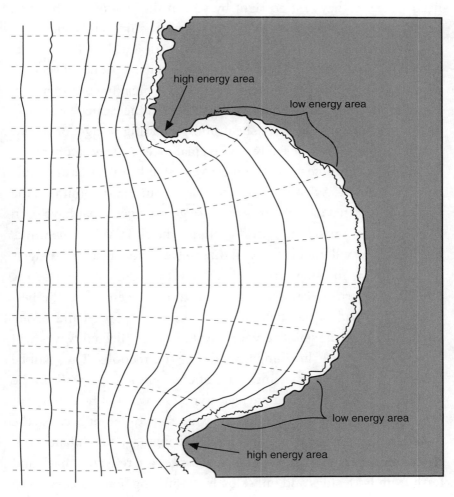

Figure 13. Wave refraction and energy distribution

Head and Deception Island in figure 14). The importance of a careful knowledge of the tide level and the charted depth cannot be overstated for circumstances such as this. A couple feet of tide change can be critical.

On the other hand, if you see a steep-sided islet near shore, but outside the surf zone, you will have a great hiding place to regroup and think things over, because there will be deep water on the shore side (see Shelter Island in figure 14). The waves will not turn into deep water so they just go right by you in the shadow of the islet. This is what most paddlers expect to happen behind an island.

Where there is no beach, you may have to deal with a different phenomenon. Wave reflection occurs when waves hit a wall and reflect back without being able to dissipate their energy by breaking onto a beach. On inland waters, this is usually a manmade object such as a bulkhead, moored barge or ship, sheet piling, floating bridge, or breakwater. Natural cliffs are usually too irregular to reflect waves coherently.

On the ocean coast, with bigger waves and swells, natural cliffs do reflect waves. As you paddle the coast, your chart should be the first indicator that danger lurks in those gentle swells that have been so easy and so much fun to paddle. Notice the cliffs. When the waves hit them they will double back on themselves, causing a very dangerous condition. You shouldn't go there. But if you do, you will find the breaking pattern indistinguishable and thus dangerous, so the best advice is to "paddle like hell!" to get out of there. Speed and strong paddle strokes will stabilize your kayak. These reflected waves will be steep and erratic, breaking from different directions. They will be difficult to lean and brace into and, of course, the shore will not be landable. Maybe, as a good navigator you just will not be there.

Wave reflection areas on inland waters are different because the waves are smaller, but they can still be challenging. Often inland wave reflection occurs in a canal where boat wakes are reflecting back and forth from both sides and only slowly dissipating. Each boat adds to the wave energy and chaos.

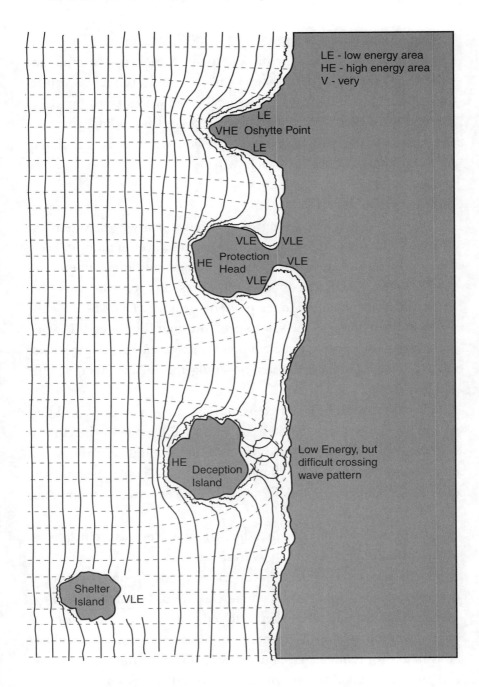

Figure 14. Several wave-refraction, energy-distribution variations

Sometimes there is a waterfront bulkhead that is way up on the beach. At low tide you may have casually launched into moderate waves from the nice beach that was in front of it, but when you returned at high tide there were strong reflected waves at the bulkhead and no visible beach. Even if you are successful at landing where the waves impact the bulkhead, next time you won't be so indifferent about bulkheads above the beach, will you?

Waves and Current

Current has a simple, but strong, effect on waves. When the current is moving in the same direction as the waves, it tends to make them speed up and stretch out, making water conditions calmer. Conversely, when the current opposes the waves' progress, the waves become much steeper, often to the point of breaking. That's because the waves are still going at the same speed through the water, but when the speed of the opposing current is subtracted, they are going slower relative to land. This crowds them closer together, making them steeper and less stable.

It pays to watch the currents and use a nautical chart and current prediction tables where possible, since a change in the current will result in a change in paddling conditions. Paddlers have gotten into serious trouble when a "sudden storm" hit. People on shore saw no weather change; the paddlers were simply experiencing a predictable change in the currents.

Current tables tell you what the current will do at specific places. The information comes from government sources, including the National Oceanographic and Atmospheric Administration (NOAA) but is also available from several commercial sources (usually in a more specific and readable form). Typically, current tables are for strategic points, with corrections for other points in the region. They will not be available for remote areas, but using them where they are available will give you a good feel for predicting for other areas what the currents will be like, or at least where they will be strong.

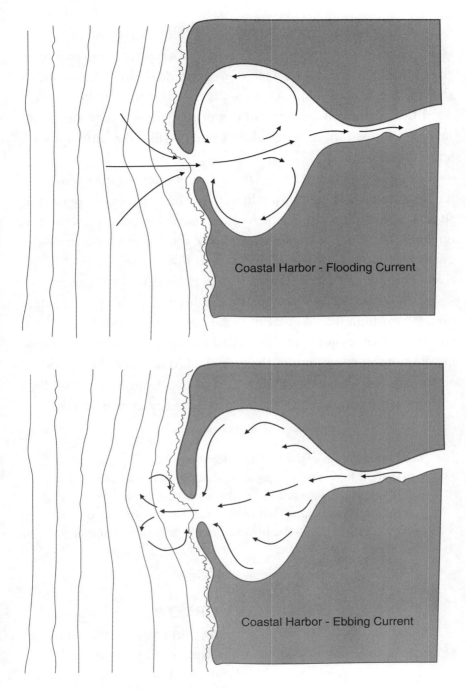

Figure 15. Natural harbors and current

Natural harbors are usually river mouths. They combine all the elements of currents, waves and beaches. At a typical ocean harbor or river mouth, you will have a jetty on each side of the entrance and a shallow bar just offshore. This results in tidal currents flowing toward the opening along both shores of the jetties. Many jetties are sandbars formed by the prevailing currents (like the sand spits referred to on page 72).

On a flood current, water flows from all directions toward the harbor entrance. Then it flows through the bay and backs up into the river. It also eddies around the bay and back along shore toward the opening (fig. 15). On an ebb current, the water flows from throughout the bay toward the entrance. It also flows from the backed up river. This increased flow causes stronger ebb than flood current.

Timing is critical when entering or leaving a harbor. The safest time is near high tide. At that time the water is deepest over the bar and the current is going in the same direction as the waves, making for the calmest conditions at the entrance. At low tide the waves are cresting as they cross the shallow area of the entrance bar, colliding with the river current and creating more difficult conditions.

TIP: Make copies of the tide table for your trip. Using clear, wide transparent tape, seal a copy to your deck where you can read it from the cockpit. Tape another to the top of your camera box. Seal a couple more by taping both sides and pass them out to your paddling buddies. Put one in your paddle jacket and another in your shirt pocket.

WIND AND CURRENT

Wind and current complicate navigation and kayak handling. They cause drift that will slow you down, speed you up, or deflect you from your course. You will find it difficult to accurately incorporate that drift into your navigation techniques. In addition to giving you problems with navigation, wind and current can make boat handling very challenging. In fact, wind and waves are more of a kayak-handling problem than a navigating problem. You are more likely to go off course because you need to turn into the wind for stability or because your kayak tends to turn into the wind, than because you are blown off course.

Navigating in these conditions requires planning your route so that you get a comfortable angle to the wind, or perhaps even waiting out extreme conditions ashore. Sometimes navigating in the wind means selecting a route where wind effects are minimized. Obviously, where you can use a landmass to block the wind, conditions will be calmer; you can follow the shore in the lee of the land.

It is very difficult to estimate wind drift, because it varies with type of kayak, the load weight, whether you have a deck load, wave conditions and, of course, the force and angle of the wind. When you find you need to correct for the actual wind drift, try compensating by setting a course 10 degrees into the wind. Then check as you go to see how it is working (see Confirming Your Course, page 68).

MAKING THE POINT

Currents form a very helpful pattern at a point, as figure 16, in the next chapter, shows. Upcurrent from the point, the currents offshore and along shore flow toward the point. Then the shore flow runs off the point and away from shore. On the downcurrent side of the point an eddy forms and flows back toward the point. The result is that, regardless of the direction of the main current, the flow along shore is toward the point.

If you have the skills, the *elegant way to round a point* from the eddy side, is to sprint up the eddy, then lean away from shore and the oncoming current as you cross the eddy line. At the same time, sweep and use your rudder to turn into the current and sprint around the point. If you are not skilled at kayak handling, the *quickest way to tip over* is to sprint up the eddy, then lean away from shore and the oncoming current as you cross the eddy line. At the same time, sweep and use your rudder to turn into the current and sprint around the point.

The *safest way to round a point* is to cross the eddy line at a slight angle, well before you get to the point, where the eddy line is weaker. Then, just sprint against the current until you are well past the point, where you can paddle back toward shore.

> **CAUTION!** Surviving the current at the point requires good boat handling skills (because you are crossing an eddyline). If you are staying close to shore because you think it's safer, you will be crossing the eddyline at its sharpest location. A tipover will usually deposit you in the current that carries you swiftly away from land just when you need its refuge. You will have to do a deep-water rescue if that happens.

CROSSING TECHNIQUES

After you start your crossing, you will need to
check your course and make corrections.

Think of open water as just something you have to cross to get to another interesting and friendly shoreline. A kayak is a very capable open-water craft and, in the hands of a competent paddler, quite safe well offshore. In truth, however, open-water crossings are usually boring. If you've done a crossing that turned out to be a terrifying or "Zen" experience, your planning and execution were probably faulty. The principal attraction of a long crossing is usually just the bragging rights for having accomplished the challenging feat.

In starting your crossing, the point is the point: no matter what crossing technique you will be using, it will be best to start your crossing from the point, when one is available. Right at the point the current, and possibly the wind, is intensified, but at least it is going in the actual direction you have to deal with on your crossing. On either

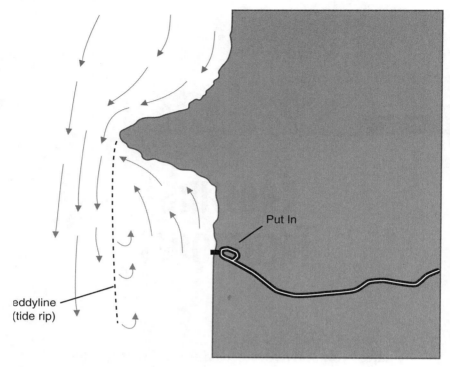

Figure 16. Currents always flow toward a point

side of the point, current flows toward the point, so paddling to it is usually easy.

Don't let the eddy fake you out. Look at figure 16. If you start your crossing at the put-in and do not notice the eddy, you will compensate for the eddy, thinking it's the current. This will make your crossing difficult, and will land you too far left along the far shore. You will have forfeited the advantage of working upstream in the eddy and taking its free ride to the point

FERRIES—THEY COST TOO MUCH

There are numerous books and articles covering ferrying, a method of combining the heading and speed of your boat with the direction and speed of the current so that you cross in a straight line to your destination. Figure 17 shows how a ferry works. Ferrying in mild current works fine, but in strong current it will be a flawed technique for several reasons. First, current is extremely variable, making predictions imprecise; you will have to constantly vary your ferry angle if you want to maintain a straight route in variable current. This is very difficult to do. Second, the faster the current, the slower your progress will be across the channel ; this will lengthen your time away from shore and expose you to traffic or other hazards. Third,

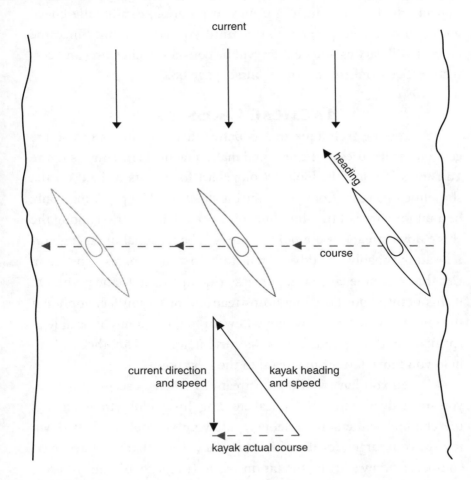

Figure 17. Ferrying: guess and correct as you go.

you cannot ferry across current that is faster than your paddling speed. All this makes ferrying practical only in mild current.

However, if you are going to ferry anyway, because of the variable current it will be easier to guess a correction and try it, than to calculate a correction. A 20-degree heading is a good initial guess; 45 degrees is usually way too much, so start your ferry by heading into the current about 20 degrees. Note that your heading (fig. 17) is the direction in which you point your kayak, not necessarily the direction in which you want to go. As you progress, continually check your route and keep correcting it until you get it right. Since the current will vary as you go, you will be constantly checking and correcting. See Confirming Your Course, page 68.

TACTICAL CROSSING

A crossing technique that is better than ferrying is to use the geographic features of the area and make a tactical crossing, as figure 18 shows. To do this, look at your chart for points of land on the shoreline upstream from your starting position. The point may only be a minor curve of the shoreline, but, as explained earlier, along the shore downstream of the point there will be minimal opposing current and probably an eddy current to help your progress upstream. Use this shoreline current for an easy ride upstream to the point. Or, if this point is not far enough upstream to make you feel confident the crossing will get you where you want to go, you might be able to sprint around the point, against its current, and find another eddy to help you move farther upstream to the next point.

When you have worked upstream as much as seems practical, you are ready to start your tactical crossing. Just paddle straight across the channel while simultaneously allowing yourself to drift down toward your target. Ideally, after a bit you will see that you have overcompensated by starting too far upstream (that's good), and you will be able to turn somewhat downstream and paddle directly and swiftly to your destination.

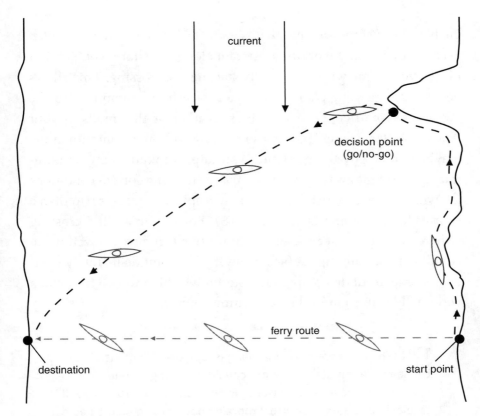

current

decision point
(go/no-go)

ferry route

destination

start point

Figure 18. Comparison of tactical crossing and ferrying

Even if you drift past your target, it will probably be easier to make up for the drift at the far shore than it would have been to try to compensate during the crossing. Just paddle back to the target using the far shore's eddies. Sometimes you may not be able to move upstream to a point to start a crossing. In that case you will have no choice but to make up all your drift along the far shore. It all depends on the geography of the area, but be sure you have fully researched the places to cross before you choose one that can offer no shoreline help.

In any case, a tactical crossing done by working upstream along the shoreline, starting from a point, paddling straight across, and correcting along the far shore is still better than trying to ferry across for several reasons. First, unlike crossing with a ferry, the tactical crossing enables you to cross current that is going faster than you can paddle. Second, by initially working upstream along the shore, you get part of the work done without actually starting the crossing. This allows you to change your plans before you have fully committed to the crossing, should conditions such as weather or the minds of your fellow paddlers change (getting something without a commitment—maybe that's a guy thing). Third, you improve your safety by minimizing your time away from shore. In fact, in strong current conditions a longer-distance tactical crossing may result in a quicker trip than a shorter ferry crossing (as in figure 18). Fourth, on a blind crossing (where you cannot see the other shore) this tactic works well when combined with aiming off (see below), where you deliberately over-compensate or undercompensate, but know which way to turn when you finally gain sight of the destination shore.

TIP: When you are crossing to a passage that is not visible because the landmasses overlap, consider veering to one side so you can see down the passage. Even though the crossing will take a little longer, it is a great morale booster to actually be able to see your destination.

CONFIRMING YOUR COURSE

The hardest part of paddling in current is in knowing the direction and speed you are actually traveling, because these differ from the direction and speed you are paddling. This will be obvious along shore; however, away from shore you have to constantly check your position and progress. There are several ways to do that.

Checking Your Course With Your Paddle

Checking your course (your actual direction of travel) is easy when you are attempting a straight route from start to destination. Simply hold the shaft of your paddle close to your face and sight down the shaft toward your starting point. Without moving the paddle, turn your head and look down the shaft in the other direction. That end of the paddle is now pointing at where you are actually going. If the paddle is pointing to the right of your destination, you are going too far right. Just veer left and keep checking with your paddle until you get it right. Don't let the ease of this technique make you doubt its usefulness. Once you try it a few times, you'll start using it routinely and frequently. See figure 19 for an illustration of how this is done.

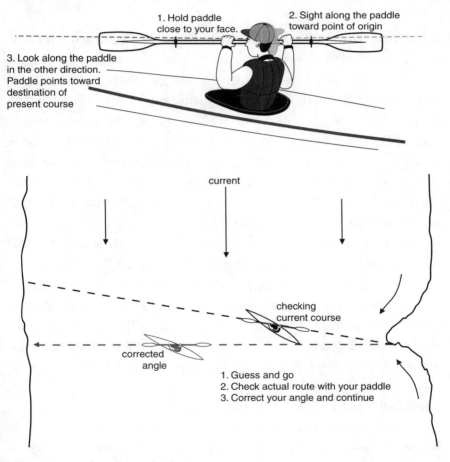

Figure 19. Checking your course (direction of travel) with your paddle

Checking Your Course With Your Compass

If you know the bearing of your destination (this is chart prepa-ration, remember?), you can use the compass to check your course. Just keep checking the bearing of your destination from where you are along the crossing route. If you use a deck-mounted compass, temporarily point your kayak at your destination to get its bearing; with a hiking compass, you can check without deviating from your kayak heading. If the bearing to your destination is decreasing, you are going too far right. Veer a little left of your original course and con-tinue. If the bearing is increasing, compensate in the other direction.

Checking Your Course With the Reverse Azimuth Method

If you can't see your destination, you have to use the reverse azimuth technique. This is just "guess and go," then "check and cor-rect." A hand-held hiking compass works best for this. You know the desired course to your destination (280 degrees) so guess a correc-tion (20 degrees, as in figure 20) and start paddling on a 300-degree bearing. Before you get out of sight of your launch site, turn around and use your hand compass to check the direction back to it. If you are on course, it will be 180 degrees (the reciprocal) from the desired course to your destination. (You marked that bearing on your chart when you planned your trip, right?) If the launch site is not 180 degrees from your desired course, correct your 20-degree guess ac-cordingly. For example, when you check your reverse azimuth, if your start site is 12 degrees more than the reciprocal, your heading is 12 degrees too high, so reduce it by 12 degrees, to 288 degrees (correct your course 12 degrees left). Now continue paddling on the new head-ing and hope nothing changes as you grope blindly toward your goal.

Checking Your Course With Ranges

Using a range is an easy way to set a course or determine a line. If you can see a buoy that lines up with a shoreline feature such as a dock, you are along a line drawn from the dock to the buoy and on to

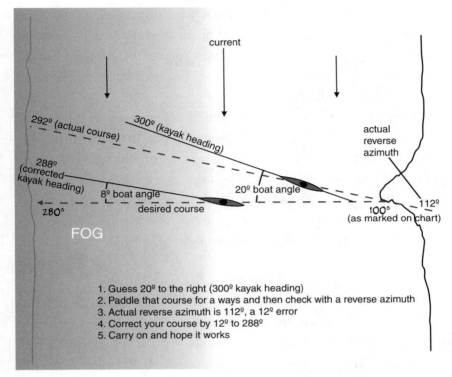

1. Guess 20º to the right (300º kayak heading)
2. Paddle that course for a ways and then check with a reverse azimuth
3. Actual reverse azimuth is 112º, a 12º error
4. Correct your course by 12º to 288º
5. Carry on and hope it works

Figure 20. Checking your course with the Reverse Azimuth method

you. This is a range. If you are paddling toward the dock and if the buoy stays in front of the dock, you are not drifting sideways to your course. If the dock is still straight ahead as you collide with the buoy, you were holding an accurate straight course (but buoy was that dumb).

Any time you are approaching a shoreline and have good visibility, you can use any background feature, such as a peak or break in a ridgeline, as a range to keep you on course. Just pick out your destination and look up from it for some identifiable mark beyond the destination point. If that far point drifts to the right, you are drifting to the right. Steer a little more left to stay on course.

Use ranges whenever you are approaching a destination from a distance. After a little practice it becomes automatic. You will always be more aware of your drift and route when using a range. It takes no time or preparation, just a little alert observation as you go. Even on a short crossing where navigation consists of just paddling over there, a range makes you more aware of wind or current drift, or even whether you are actually paddling straight.

Keep in mind that visibility problems create serious limitations for using ranges. As you approach from offshore, the foreground hills will appear larger and will hide the distant mountains, even though it seems as if a mountaintop should be a pretty reliable feature. And, as weather deteriorates, the visibility ceiling can drop quickly to conceal a high feature. If using a range for your route identification is critical, back it up by using a compass bearing as well.

AIMING OFF

If you are crossing to a long shoreline (one you can't miss), it may be easier not to compensate at all. Aiming off means you note which way the drift is, make no allowance for it and start your crossing. When you can see the opposite shore well enough to identify features, veer upstream along shore, where the current is usually weaker or you have favorable eddies, until you reach your destination. For the same reasons as the tactical crossing, this is easier, faster, and more reliable than ferrying. Consider it to be a tactical crossing with a built-in error. Aiming off and knowing in which direction you will miss the target is better that trying to hit it dead center and then wondering over whether you missed it to the right or the left.

SPITS

As you saw back in figure 16, the current along the shore at a point always flows toward the point, regardless of the direction of the main current. This is how a sand point can exist where the main current would seem to make it unlikely. Near a sand point there is usually a feeder bluff that has sand eroding off it onto the nearby beach. The waves agitate this beach sand and the current moves the sand toward the point. Meanwhile, the main current erodes the tip of the sand point, keeping it from growing infinitely, and keeping the system of bluff and point erosion in balance.

If a bulkhead, road, or other bank stabilization upsets this balance, the sand point will shrink. Many sand beaches have disappeared because of civilization's improvements. If, on the other hand, the water is shallow and conditions are right, the point will grow to become a very long point, called a sand spit. In some areas the sand spit will form a natural harbor, a breakwater made of sand, no less. Frequently a bay will be partially closed off by a spit.

As a coastal navigator, remember that these points and spits are formed by the continuous currents along the shore moving sand toward a point. When you see a sand point or spit you should think of it as a one way traffic sign as you plan your way around a bay. Even when you have no documentation to show you the current's direction, you can tell the direction by the direction of the spit point. (Note: on lakes and other areas where there is no significant current, prevailing wave and wind conditions create the spits, not current, and the current along the spits will be negligible).

> **CAUTION!** Even if the current along the spit is small, such as half a knot, don't underestimate its effect. You can fight it OK, but subtracting it or adding it to your hull speed makes a total difference of 1 knot. For example, if your hull speed is 3 knots, your gain will be 2½ knots going against the current and 3½ knots going with the current. The difference in your progress will be 1 knot, twice the actual current, in this case one third of your hull speed. At a cruise speed of 3 knots, that is a large factor if efficiency is important.

ADDITIONAL CONSIDERATIONS

There are several ways to help make navigation more comfortable. One is to have several navigators for the trip. They will help catch errors and improve accuracy and safety. If your group splits up, multiple navigators would be essential. Another way is to use your group's paddling ability and comfort level to set your course to the wind. This may be more important than the desired direction. On a crossing, you'll find it easier to keep the group together if you use speed estimates for the slowest paddler and make the slowest paddler your crossing leader.

TIP: Pencils are OK for figuring on a chart, but any note that you want to save should be with a fine-point waterproof marker or ballpoint pen.

Chapter 5

THE OTHER GUYS

The main rule of the road is this: the Little Guy (you) stays out of the way of the Big Guys (them).

As you venture forth in your kayak, you will find that there can be a lot of other boats out there and they all will be bigger than you. They are also fast and their pilots perhaps not too intelligent. After all, if they were smart they would know how much better it is to be in a kayak.

These other craft are possibly the greatest hazard to sea kayakers. Commercial cargo vessels can't maneuver or stop quickly, and recreational traffic is unpredictable and often irrational. Sailboats are accustomed to being the "Privileged Vessel" and believing others should to yield to them. Commercial boats that are towing or fishing are also given right-of-way priority. Technically, in many circumstances manually-powered vessels such as ours have right-of-way over sailing and powered craft, but the point is academic. In reality, it is up to you to stay out of everyone else's way. In confined areas and some other circumstances, it is also your legal obligation, so there is no point in being assertive.

RIGHT-OF-WAY VS. REALITY

How can a kayaker win by asserting his rights, but being involved in an accident?

There are some important rules, but the main rule of the road is this: the Little Guy (you) stays out of the way of the Big Guys (them). Just imagine you are driving downtown in heavy traffic. A pigeon flies up in front of you. Do you swerve into the bus next to you or do you hit the pigeon? Now think about driving a cumbersome tanker down a channel as a kayak darts out in front of you. Is there any point in driving your tanker onto the rocks in a feeble, and probably futile, attempt to avoid the kayak when you probably wouldn't actually hit it anyway? Most commercial vessels are meant to have the whole ocean to maneuver in, and they are not capable of avoiding kayakers and other agile traffic in confined areas. And by law, they don't have to.

While kayakers should have the right-of-way over recreational sailboats and powerboats, how can a kayaker win by asserting his rights, but being involved in an accident? Sailors are used to having their own way, since they have right-of-way over powerboats, but they are also used to watching out for powerboats and other big guys. Furthermore, they often can't see what is in front of them or approaching from the side because of their sails. In addition, both powerboats and sailboats have difficulty seeing kayaks, because they ride low in the water.

Sailors are dealing with the same elements kayakers are, and often barely making it. When they are beating into the wind they work for every foot. Even if you have the right-of-way, if you force them to fall off their line, they will do so only at the last minute. Since their visibility is poor with all that cloth hanging in front of the skipper, you probably do not want to force the issue, only to find out at the last instant that they don't actually see you. There is not much point in being dead right. There is not much point in being dead, right? If you are that belligerent, there is not much point in being. Dead Right!

Power boaters are another animal altogether: common advice among some kayakers concerning recreational power boaters is to assume they are drunk and angry, so stay out of their way. In many areas the only qualification to pilot a large, fast powerboat is a down payment and good credit. Although most owners are very responsible and courteous, there are enough who are not to make avoidance your best defense. Power boaters are often erratic in their behavior, but some of their preferences are predictable. Many are taking the most direct line between their start and tonight's raft-up party. If you

Kayaker wannabes think they can land anywhere, too. Photo by Lee Moyer

look at your chart for the most direct routes to moorage, that is where you get most of the powerboat traffic. If you pick a route around the other side of the island, or slightly off the main route, you see far fewer bozo boaters. Few power boaters are out to enjoy a casual trip. Their enjoyment often comes from having the shortest elapsed time and best stocked bar. Often they are inattentive or distracted while under way. One large fast cruiser once hit a Washington State ferry broadside in mid-day. The power boater said he didn't see the 400-foot-long, 5-story-high, white ship. The only reassuring point for kayakers is that we are a smaller target, so we are harder to hit. Books on safety suggest bright colored kayaks, paddles and PFDs. It could help, but not as much as staying out of the way as much as possible.

Commercial craft are the easiest to deal with. They are under the control of experienced pilots who probably know better than you what should be done next. Fortunately, commercial traffic is predictable, because in many areas of commercial activity, such as Puget Sound, Long Island Sound, and Chesapeake Bay, they are following known and noted traffic lanes and are under the control of a Vessel Traffic System, the same as aircraft in a controlled air space. Their travel usually is in designated lanes that are marked on your chart. The straight-line routes, separation zones and turning points are well defined so you can tell what the ship is doing and will be doing. If you are crossing a channel with commercial traffic, plan well ahead. Even though you have plenty of time to decide whether you will go in front of or behind that freighter, make your intentions obvious well in advance so the pilot knows he doesn't have to consider avoidance procedures.

Tugs without a tow are deceiving; they look slow, but they really are fast and agile. They also make a very large wake for a ship so small. On the other hand, tugs with a tow are slow and unmaneuverable. They are deceiving, too. Because their towline will be under water, you might think there is no tow. You must look way behind the tug, as the tow will usually be big, quiet and much farther back than you would expect. At night it's even worse; the tug will have two or three lights lined up vertically on its mast if it has a tow, but the tow itself will be poorly lit. Lights aligned like that are a major danger signal. Often, the only thing you will see is a dark area moving along shore where the shore lights seem to go out and then on again as the tow goes by.

Charts also show ferryboat routes. Ferryboats differ from other commercial traffic in that they are often faster, and take a crossing route rather than follow a channel. They are also much more agile than most other commercial traffic; however, it is still up to you to stay out of their way.

Fishing boats that are actually fishing move slowly and need lots of room. Trollers have lines extending from booms off the sides of the boat, and often have additional lines from a float trailing well behind the boat. Gillnetters have long nets with floats along the top. You can paddle across these nets safely and without doing harm— but, just hope the fisherman agrees with you. Stay away from purse seiners who are pulling their nets around with a small powerboat to encircle the fish, sea lions, and sea kayakers, all of which they will sort out later. There are also trawlers, shrimp and lobster trap tenders, and numerous other types of fishing boats. Unless you are very sure of what is going on, stay well away from them. Of course, a good forager keeps ten bucks handy and a smile on his face, just in case there's something available for dinner. It sometimes pays to get up-close and personal.

COLLISION COURSE OR NOT?

Are you on a collision course? If you aren't moving, and the other guy is coming at you, you are! If he is straight ahead or behind you and coming at you, you are! Even a power boater knows that. But often you are just on an intersecting route, and it is a collision course only if you both reach the intersection at the same time.

Your first thought should be: "Who is that guy?" If it is a commercial ship, make your actions obvious well in advance so the pilot knows you are taking action and has time to plan. This should be done much earlier than you actually have to act to avoid the collision; you are acting early to signal the other boat. If it is a recreational boat, early action isn't as necessary, since they may not be on a consistent course anyway. Just be alert to their course changes and allow yourself time for avoidance.

On intersecting routes, it's easy to see if you are on a collision course. Just keep track of the bearing to the other boat. You can do this just by watching and noting whether the other boat is moving toward you at a constant angle off your bow, or if that angle is changing. If it doesn't change, you will collide. If the angle is decreasing, he is will pass in front of you. It might be smart to turn toward him to show that you intend to go behind him. If the angle is increasing, you are crossing in front of him. Be sure you will be able to do so with a comfortable margin of safety.

As you maintain your course, you'll find a hand-held compass very convenient to check for a collision course. Just check the direction to the other guy with your compass. If the direction doesn't change, keep the duct tape and first aid kit handy.

AVOIDANCE IS THE BEST ANSWER

Yes, all the comments about the other guys add up to one thing: stay away from them! That is not as difficult or as bad as it sounds. The best place to paddle is along shore anyway. Crossings are just a way to get to another shoreline. Usually the best route is the one that minimizes the time away from shore and doesn't use the classic ferry technique. Where it is barely deep enough to kayak, it is usually too shallow for the other guys, so you can be safe and at the same time see more wildlife. Now all you have to worry about is jet skiers and kids on shore throwing rocks (If we could just get both of those together, we'd have a self-correcting problem).

FOG AND WIND

If you really like your heartbeat high,
consider raising it with exercise, rather than
with panic.

Fog can be peaceful, soothing . . . and terrifying. The gray cover sometimes feels like a refreshing security blanket as you glide along the misty shoreline. It can be addictive. Or, your group is offshore and listening to a large motor. Each person faces the noise to hear better. Each is facing a different direction. But at least it is no longer getting louder. Wait a minute! It *is* getting louder! If you really like your heartbeat this high, consider raising it with exercise, rather than with panic.

Some areas, such as New England, have frequent fog problems, and paddlers there must learn to deal with it. However, most areas do not have much fog, but may have weather conditions of rain and spray that are equally as bad. On a crossing of several miles, rain alone can create a blind crossing condition. Most instruction on navigation emphasizes blind navigation techniques such as dead reckoning because these techniques are the only way to navigate to a point when you are unable to see. Since they are also mathematical, they seem to be the learned thing to do. However, a tactical crossing, or use of techniques such as aiming off or reverse azimuth are usually more practical in bad conditions.

WHAT IS FOG?

All fog is formed the same way: air cools to the point where it can no longer hold all of its water vapor and the vapor condenses out as small droplets that are so small they are held in suspension and do not fall. If they get big enough to fall, they are called rain. Warm air can hold more moisture than cold air, which is why we use warm air to dry things. If it cools, the water comes back. The fraction of the total capability of the air that is actually used to absorb the vapor is called the relative humidity. Fifty per cent relative humidity means the air holds half of what it could hold. You get that sticky, clammy feeling when the air is holding about all the water vapor it can hold, and nothing will dry. As the temperature drops and the ability of the air to hold moisture decreases, eventually the temperature reaches a point where the air can hold no more moisture. That temperature is called the dew point. Dew will form on items that are cooler than the air. Typically, as surfaces radiate their heat away in the evening, they reach a point where they cool the air they touch and dew forms. When the air itself reaches that point, fog forms. Thus, fog will form in the cool of the night, be there in the morning and maybe burn off as the day warms up.

This type of fog is called radiation fog because it forms as the heat radiates away and the air cools. It typically forms in still or gentle breeze conditions, because strong wind would mix up the air and keep the ground air from cooling enough. However, this does not mean you will have only calm conditions with fog. Sea fog is formed offshore and brought in by wind. You can often see it coming. It will be a big wall, called a fog bank. It can be brought in by very strong winds, which will not die quickly, and the sea fog does not burn off.

SAFETY IN FOG AND WIND

If there is a significant breeze from the ocean, beware: it may get worse and sea fog could last for days.

In foggy conditions your weather radio will be invaluable in helping you decide whether to launch in the morning. That makes your weather radio your whether radio. It is possible to predict when

Are those guys safe in this weather? Photo courtesy Rippin' Productions—Jock Bradley

radiation fog will burn off. Although sea fog can be reliably predicted, predicting how far inland it will go and how long it will last is not so reliable. If you are getting up in fog on a calm day and yesterday's weather was good, probably the fog will burn off; the radio weather person will predict clearing. But if there is a significant breeze from the ocean, beware: it may get worse and sea fog could last for days.

Of course, your weather radio is great for checking other expected paddling conditions, too, primarily wind. Often, the wind you feel is not what the weather radio says you have, but the actual conditions are not nearly as important as the trend. You may think you know whether you want to paddle in the wind you have, but you can make a safer decision if you also know whether the wind is going to increase or decrease. The weather radio will tell you if a low-pressure system is moving in, and what the general tendency of your paddling conditions will be.

TIP: Before you return to an area, buy another set of charts and transfer all your notes to that chart also. Keep that one as a reference; your other one won't last forever.

Chapter 7

NIGHT PADDLING

If there are no lights on shore, it will be very difficult to tell where you are going

Night paddling is almost mystical. It is beautiful, intellectual, and indirect. Where, by day, you see the details of what is around you, by night you perceive indirect clues. By day, you see a barge go by; however, on a dark night you only see a shoreline area where the lights go out for a time and then reappear. By day, you follow a shoreline easily. On a dark night you may be way offshore because you mistake the reflection of the skyline for the shoreline. Much can go wrong on a night paddle, but the reward of paddling on a beautiful night is almost a religious experience.

PROBLEMS IN THE DARK

For night paddling, your first consideration is, "How dark is it?" Paddling near a city or on a moonlight night is not much more difficult than paddling in the daytime. It will be a little harder to see the other guys, keep your group together, and identify landmarks, but you will have the advantage of the incidental lights on shore and of navigation lights, which are indicated on your chart. In fact, you will see cities just by their reflected glow in the sky, even it they are not in your line of sight. On some long crossings to inhabited islands, paddlers time their arrival for darkness because the lights of the island are visible for a greater distance than the island itself would be in the daylight.

If it is very dark because of no moon or overcast sky, it is also hard to see your fellow paddlers. You will want to have a marking light on the back of each kayak or kayaker. It is also best to keep the group small. If there are no lights on shore, it will be very difficult to tell where you are going; it may seem logical to have a lit compass, or a headlamp to see your compass, but it will still be difficult to maintain a course. Too often you will have to veer off your compass course just to see that everyone is still together. With more than two or three paddlers, this will make maintaining a compass course almost impossible. You will also find yourself losing touch with the other paddlers, or colliding with them. Either way, you are distracted from your course. So, on very dark nights, it is best to limit your paddling to confined areas or to times when shoreline lights are reliable.

TIP: Learn a couple of simple magic tricks. They are fun around a campfire.

LIGHTING THE WAY

You are not required to use running lights on a kayak, but the Coast Guard requires that you carry three emergency flares and a strong white light. The flares are your distress signals. The strong light is to be readily available to shine at an approaching craft to avoid a collision. Usually your first attempt to be noticed by another craft should be for all group members to shine their lights on one another, so the oncoming craft can see, identify, and count everyone. If that is not bright enough, shine all your lights at the oncoming craft. Be careful when he shines back. Not only will you be chasing brightly colored balloons around the bay for a few minutes, but you'll also wonder if you just received instant sunburn.

Unlike kayaks, power boats and sailboats under way at night will have running lights: red and green lights toward the bow and a white light higher and aft. See figures 21 and 22. The red light is the port running light visible from dead ahead to just aft of abeam; the green is the starboard running light. If you find the combinations of port/starboard, red/green and left/right hard to keep straight, just re-member the shorter words of each pair go together and the longer words go together. Port, red and left are on one side; starboard, green and right are on the other.

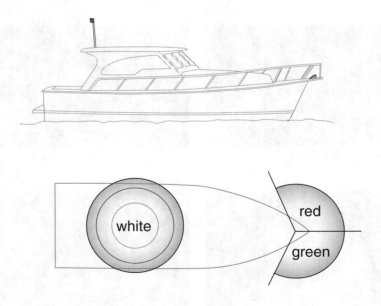

Figure 21. Night running lights on power boats and sailboats

The white light is visible from all directions. Large ships will have two white lights, one well ahead of the other. If you see red on the right, green on the left and a white light directly above, immediately confirm that all the paddlers in your group have included you in their wills and then paddle like hell to get out of there. If you see a green light, with a white light above it and to the left, you are to the right of the other guy and he is moving to your right. If you only see a white light and it is moving, you are somewhere behind him and he is moving away from you. A single white light could also be marking an anchored craft. He has the right-of-way, so yield to him.

If you see a boat with running lights and a vertical array of two or three lights on the mast, beware! That is a boat with a tow. A two-light tow is smaller than a three-light tow, but who cares? They are both a lot bigger than you. The tow will probably be poorly lit, far behind, and quiet, so give it plenty of room. On the Pacific coast it is

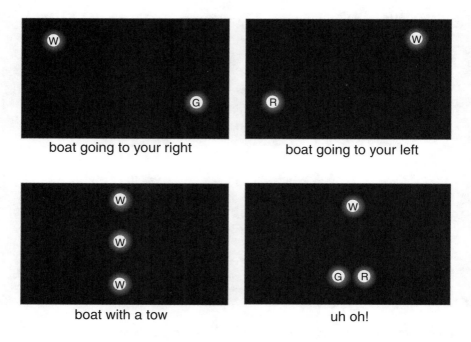

boat going to your right

boat going to your left

boat with a tow

uh oh!

Figure 22. The other guy at night

not unusual for a tugboat captain to look aft at the break of dawn and see a powerboat parked on his log boom. When a kayak collides with a tow, it will not be humorous. Of course, that is only speculation, since no one will ever know what happened.

NIGHT MAGIC

If, after all this, you are asking yourself why you should even consider paddling at night, just wait for one of those magical nights of phosphorescence, when your paddle strokes sparkle, spooked fish leave glowing contrails, and you crash into your buddy because you are both gawking at the incredible light show under your kayaks. Once you see the kelp strands glow like neon lights, you'll be hooked on night paddling, too.

Glossary

bearing: The direction toward an object or location.

charts: Marine maps.

The Coastal Pilot: A book of coastal features put out by a governmental agency to help ship navigators, but also useful to kayakers. It is called Sailing Directions in some countries.

compass: A magnetic gadget with a needle or arrow that usually points at the magnetic north Pole.

compass rose: A round, segmented figure printed on a chart, indicating magnetic and true directions. The outer scale is true, the inner scale magnetic. You compare directions on the chart with the rose to identify a direction.

course: A route or direction of travel.

courser: A clear plastic film with parallel lines printed on it for transferring directions from one place on a chart to another.

current: The horizontal movement of water. Predictions are along the surface.

declination: See variation.

ebb current: Current that is flowing toward the sea.

flood current: Current that is moving inland, flooding the land.

fog (radiation fog): Fog caused by lowering temperatures, usually in calm conditions.

fog (sea fog): Fog formed offshore and carried to land by wind.

heading: The direction in which your kayak is pointing. It is not your course unless there is no drift caused by current or wind.

knot: One nautical mile per hour. Knot is a unit of speed, not distance. Saying knots per hour is like saying miles per hour per hour.

lights (running lights): those used to identify craft and their operation at night.

lights (navigation lights): shore line markers to aid in nighttime navigation.

mile (nautical mile): One minute of latitude, 6080 feet, 1.15 statute miles.

NOAA: National Oceanographic and Atmospheric Administration, the U.S. Government source of charts, weather information, river flows, etc.

north (magnetic north): Where your compass needle actually points. The magnetic north pole is somewhere north of Hudson Bay.

north (true north): The direction of the north pole, which is on the centerline about which the earth rotates. Straight up on most charts and maps.

parallel rulers: Two straight edges kept parallel by connecting, pivoting links. By "walking" the instrument across the sheet by holding one of the straightedges in place, then the other, directions are transferred from one place on the chart to another.

PFD: Personal Flotation Device (life vest)

range: A line or course along a line that is determined by aligning with two distant features, such as a shoreline building and a mountain in the background, or one feature and a compass direction.

reef: A shallow area in relatively deep water.

Sailing Directions: Another term for *The Coastal Pilot.*

shoal: Shallow area or reef.

tide: The rise and fall of the water level. Low tide is the level at which the tide stops falling and starts rising. High tide is the level at which the tide stops rising and starts falling. There are usually two high and two low tides per 24-hour day. Each tide occurs about an hour later each day.

tide (neap tide): The less extreme tide occurring when the sun and moon are not opposed or aligned. The opposite of spring tide.

tides (spring tide): The most extreme tides of the lunar cycle, occurring when the sun and moon are aligned.

variation (a.k.a. declination on maps): The difference between magnetic north and true north on the chart you are using. It is printed on the compass rose. This is the correction you apply to your compass to get true directions from magnetic directions. Since this is a frequent source of error, it's usually best to apply it to the true directions while you plan your trip at home and use magnetic directions, which you read directly from your compass, while you are out paddling.

SUGGESTED READING

Burch, David; *Fundamentals of Kayak Navigation*, 3 ed. The Globe Pequot Press, Guilford, CT, 1999.

Dowd, John: *Sea Kayaking*, 4 ed. University of Washington Press, Seattle, WA, 1997.

Johnson, Shelley; *Sea Kayaking: A Woman's Guide*. Ragged Mountain Press, Camden, ME 1998

Washburne, Randel; *Coastal Kayakers Manual*, 3 ed. Globe Pequot Press, Guilford, CT, 1998.

Index

INDEX

INDEX

THE AUTHOR

L ee Moyer is, as he puts it, "a recovering Boeing engineer," having
worked there for a few years before experiencing first hand "the
Boeing Bust" in the early seventies. In 1974 he and his former wife,
Judy, turned their avocation into their vocation, starting their Seattle-
area store, Pacific Water Sports.

In addition to the store, Lee is a kayak designer and manufac-
turer, a kayak instructor, and an activist in Seattle area environmen-
tal, water access and boating safety issues. He is a long-time director
of the Puget Soundkeeper Alliance, which works with businesses and
the government to clean up the Puget Sound environment.

In thirty years of paddling, Lee has kayaked the coasts in parts
of Central America, Mexico, Maine, Lake Superior, British Columbia,
Alaska, and Washington state.